the lord's prayer

THE LORD'S PRAYER

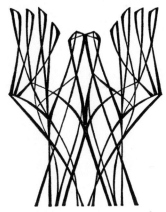

An Interpretation

CHARLES L. ALLEN

FLEMING H. REVELL COMPANY

Illustrations by Ismar David

POWER IN PRAYER

THE LORD'S PRAYER CAN BE SAID IN JUST FIFTEEN
seconds; even for a large congregation to repeat it
slowly takes only half a minute. Yet Jesus would spend
half the night praying that same prayer. Today there
are over five hundred million people who can say the
Lord's Prayer, but very few ever learn to pray it. The
power comes, not in the saying, but in the praying of
the prayer.

Praying is not saying words. Words merely form the
frame on which the temple of thought is built. The
power of the Lord's Prayer is not in the words, but
rather in the pattern of thinking in which our minds
are formed. The Bible tells us, "Be ye transformed by
the renewing of your mind" (ROMANS 12:2). When
our thoughts begin to flow in the channels of the Lord's
Prayer our minds do become new, and we are transformed. To the extent that we think the thoughts of
Christ, to that same extent do we have the power of
Christ.

CHARLES L. ALLEN

the lord's prayer

OUR FATHER WHICH ART IN HEAVEN,
HALLOWED BE THY NAME.
THY KINGDOM COME.
THY WILL BE DONE IN EARTH,
AS IT IS IN HEAVEN.
GIVE US THIS DAY OUR DAILY BREAD.
AND FORGIVE US OUR DEBTS,
AS WE FORGIVE OUR DEBTORS.
AND LEAD US NOT INTO TEMPTATION,
BUT DELIVER US FROM EVIL:
FOR THINE IS THE KINGDOM,
AND THE POWER,
AND THE GLORY,
FOR EVER.
AMEN.

our father
which art in heaven

"OUR FATHER WHICH ART IN HEAVEN," JESUS
tells us to pray. If we had only those six words we
would have the Lord's Prayer. The other sixty
words Jesus gave in the prayer are by way of explanation. Learn really to pray that first phrase and you
need go no further.

The word "Father" is a definition of God. For
us it is an imperfect definition, because we as fathers
are imperfect. A preacher who worked with boys in
a slum area said he could not refer to God as a
father. When those boys thought of father they
pictured men who frequently were drunk and beat
their mothers. We all put into that word the im-
perfections of our own fathers.

Thus Jesus could not use merely the term
"Father." He must add, "which art in heaven."
That phrase is not there to locate God or to tell us
where God lives. Somehow, we have made up our
minds that heaven is far distant. In one of our most

8

beloved hymns, "The Old Rugged Cross," we sing, "He will call me some day to that home far away." And we think of God as being in that home far away. That is all wrong and not according to the teachings of Jesus. God is as near as the air you breathe.

Heaven is synonymous with perfection. Jesus might have said, "Our perfect Father," and it would have been the same thing. And when you think of the term "Father" immediately you think not of easy indulgence but of authority. In the very act of recognizing a Father you are making yourself a son. And the Father has the right of command over His sons.

Therefore, you surrender your own will to His will. It is not what you want but what He wants that becomes your controlling thought. We recognize the fact that God has established a moral order. Man does not create his laws, he merely discovers God's laws. By obedience to those laws we learn with Dante, "His will is our peace."

On the other hand, to fail to recognize the sovereignty of God is to fail in all of life. The seal of one of the Waldensian churches pictures an anvil and a number of broken hammers, with the motto:

"Hammer away, ye hostile hands! Your hammers break; God's anvil stands." So, until you can say "Father," you need not attempt to pray further.

However, Father means more than ruler or lawgiver or judge. Father signifies a rule of love, it puts mercy into the very heart of judgment. Because love begets love, thus our response to God becomes not one of fear, but of true sonship. St. Paul said it well: "For ye have not received the spirit of bondage again to fear; but ye have received the Spirit of adoption, whereby we cry, Abba, Father" (ROMANS 8:15).

"Heavenly Father" means not only authority and love, it also means holiness. Once, as Isaiah walked into the church, he heard the seraphims singing, "Holy, holy, holy, is the Lord of hosts." When he saw the spotless purity of God he was convinced and convicted of his own unrighteousness to the point he cried, "Woe is me! for I am undone; because I am a man of unclean lips," and he fell before God in repentance and consecration (ISAIAH 6:5).

Why is it we close our eyes when we pray? Perhaps the reason is to shut out the world in order to be able to give our complete attention to God. However, true prayer opens our eyes. To pray, "Father," means to recognize our sonship, but it also means to recognize our brotherhood. A young man came in to see me recently. He had spent two years in prison. Sometimes we do not realize the blessings of society until we are shut away from it. He said to me, "I do not want much in life. I only want to belong again." "To belong," that is what we all want. But to pray, "Our Father," means to remove all boundaries and barriers and to make every one of us a child of God.

In this first phrase of the Lord's Prayer is summed up the Christian life. The word "Father" expresses our faith. Not only does it mean that we believe in a God, but also the very word describes Him. *"In heaven" includes all our hopes.* Meaning perfection, the word "heaven" signifies the quality of life toward which Christians are striving. "Be ye therefore perfect," said Christ, "even as your Father which is in heaven is perfect" (MATTHEW 5:48).

Man is never satisfied with himself. He is ever striving upward and onward. He can bear the failures of the past and present because he hopes to do better tomorrow. When a friend was looking over the work of William W. Story, the famous sculptor, he asked: "For which of your carvings do you care

11

the most?" To which the sculptor replied: "I care most for the statue I'm going to carve next."

The word "our" means all inclusive love. Without that, prayer is futile. There is no such thing as a solitary religion, because unless we say "brother," we cannot say "Father." Ernest Crosby in his poem "The Search" says it:

> No one could tell me where my soul might be;
> I sought for God, but God eluded me;
> I sought my brother out and found all three.

Faith—Hope—Love, they are all included.

How it would change my life to really pray, "Our Father which art in heaven." It would throw me on my knees in some Gethsemane in complete obedience to His will. It would lead me to sacrifice my life in serving and seeking to save my fellow man. Most important, it would bring God into my soul.

Then, no matter what might happen, in complete confidence I could pray, even as my Lord prayed, "Father, into thy hands I commend my spirit" (LUKE 23:46). Thus I would have the assurance that I could leave the results of my life in God's hands, knowing that even out of my seeming defeats in life would come glorious triumph. That out of the graves of my life would come resurrections and I would sing with the Apostle, "O death, where is thy sting? O grave, where is thy victory? . . . Thanks be to God, which giveth us the victory through our Lord Jesus Christ" (I CORINTHIANS 15:55,57).

Often I visit the cemetery where my father is laid to rest. I like to go and stand at his grave and think about him. I always feel uplifted.

I think about how good he was to me. How he gave all he had in a material way to his children, not just food and clothes and the necessities of life. Also balls and bats and the things with which boys like to play. He was happy in making us happy. I think about each night he would pray for us, one by one. There is a recording of his voice in my mind as he prays, "Lord, bless Charles. May he grow up to be a good man." "Bless Stanley," he would say. "Bless John—Grace—Blanche—Sarah—Frances." He would have a special prayer for each of us.

Standing there at his grave, I think of his deep honesty, of his high standards. I think of his humility. He was very unpretentious, never seeking much for himself. Our parsonage was usually next

13

door to the church, where day after day people came seeking help. I think of how he always shared what we had, never turning anybody away. Sometimes I forget about time as I stand there thinking about him.

So I feel I understand, at least in a very small way, something of what Jesus meant when He told us to pray, "Our Father." Again and again, our Lord would go out into the mountains alone to pray. He would often stay all night. On one occasion He even stayed forty days, forgetting time, even forgetting to eat. There in the quietness He would think about His Father.

And He tells us that is the way to pray, "Our Father which art in heaven." We are not asking God for something; instead we open the way for the inflow of God into us. Norman Vincent Peale tells of his first visit to the Grand Canyon. He met a man who had spent much time at the canyon, so he asked which trip he should take in order to see the most possible of the canyon.

The wise old man told him if he really wanted to see the canyon he should not take any of the trips at all. Instead, he should come out early in the morning and take a seat on the rim, sit there and

watch the morning pass into noontime and the noontime into afternoon, with the everchanging colors gleaming across the great canyon. Then get a quick supper and return to watch the purple twilight come over the vast abyss. The old man said that if one runs around, he merely wears himself out and misses the beauty and greatness of it all.

Well, that is what the old Prophet said about God in the long ago, "They that wait on the Lord shall renew their strength" (ISAIAH 40:31). What does it mean to "wait on the Lord"? It means to think about God, though "think" is hardly the word. To meditate better expresses it, to contemplate is still better. Or as the Psalmist put it, "Be still, and know that I am God" (46:10).

H. G. Wells said, *"Until a man has found God he begins at no beginning and works to no end."* So you are not ready to pray until first your mind has been possessed by thoughts of God. For several years now I have watched hundreds of people kneel in prayer at the altar in the closing moments of the Sunday night service. Many have told me of amazing results of those prayers.

The reason why those altar prayers are so much more meaningful for many is because they come at the close of the service. For an hour or more the sacred building has been reminding them of the person of God. The hymns, the reading of the Bible, the sermon, the presence of other worshiping people, all work together to make one aware of the nearness of God. Then, when one kneels to pray his mind is properly conditioned, his thinking is Godly. Thus his prayer is natural and real. His words and his thoughts are the same.

"Our Father which art in heaven"—when those words become real to us we become quiet and confident. As Elizabeth Cheney expresses it:

> *Said the Robin to the Sparrow,*
> *"I should really like to know*
> *Why these anxious human beings*
> *Rush about and worry so."*
> *Said the Sparrow to the Robin,*
> *"Friend, I think that it must be*
> *That they have no Heavenly Father*
> *Such as cares for you and me."*

hallowed be thy name

JESUS TEACHES US THAT THERE ARE SIX things for which man should pray. But before man can begin the other five petitions he must pray, "Hallowed be thy name." Once Moses was out on a hillside watching the sheep. He saw a bush on fire which continued to burn without burning up. After a time Moses went over to see about it.

Actually, God was in that bush, ready to reveal His will for Moses' life, but as Moses approached he heard a voice saying, "Put off thy shoes from off thy feet, for the place whereon thou standest is holy ground" (EXODUS 3:5). The meaning of this is that before God speaks to man, man must have proper respect and reverence.

Many people never think of praying except in time of crisis. That is when we have a need which we ourselves cannot meet. And our prayers concern only ourselves, what we want God to do for us. That is why so few people really pray with power. *Jesus says that first we must have God in our minds.* To "hallow" means to respect and reverence.

But notice, Jesus does not tell *us* to hallow God's name. Rather is it a prayer, which means asking God to do something that we are unable to do. Thus we are asking God to hallow His own name. Profane man can do nothing for God until first God has done something for man. Suppose an artist, even the greatest artist of all time, said, "I shall go out and paint the sky." We would laugh at him. So man cannot hallow the name of God. If you tried to blacken the sky with a tar brush, you would succeed only in getting tar over yourself. The sky would remain as it is. So what does Jesus mean by this prayer?

The emphasis is not on the word "hallow" but on "name." The Bible is a book of names. Every name has a meaning, given to reveal the character of the person. For example, the name "Jesus" means "God is Salvation." Thus the angel said to Joseph: "Thou shalt call his name Jesus: for he shall save his people from their sins" (MATTHEW 1:21).

When Andrew brought his brother to Christ the Lord said, "Thou art Simon the son of Jona." But under the influence of Christ he would become a different person. So Jesus says his name will be changed: "Thou shalt be called Cephas, which is by interpretation, A stone," something strong and unshakable (JOHN 1:42).

To know a person's name, in the Bible, was to know the person. Thus God's "name" means His nature revealed. So "Hallowed be thy name" really means, *"Reveal thyself to me, O God."* In the long ago Job asked, "Canst thou by searching find out God?" (JOB 11:7). The answer is no. Man can know God only as God chooses to reveal Himself.

Walter de la Mare asks a question that we all sometimes ask. As he prays he wonders, "Is there anybody there?" Before you can pray you must be sure there is a Somebody to hear, and be conscious of His presence.

There are several ways in which God reveals Himself. First, in His marvelous creation. "The heavens declare the glory of God; and the firmament showeth his handiwork" (PSALM 19:1). That is the first revelation God made of Himself. We stand at the seashore and are moved by the boundless expanse before us. When we remember that He can hold all the seas in "the hollow of his hand" (ISAIAH 40:12), then we see something of His power. Standing among great mountain peaks, His majesty is impressed upon us.

Jesus stood reverently before a wild "lily of the field" and saw the glory of God (MATTHEW 6:28, 29). *"Earth's crammed with heaven, and every common bush afire with God,"* sings Elizabeth Barrett Browning. We look into the heavens and

20

see the infiniteness of God, at a tiny snowflake and see His perfection. The sunset opens our eyes to His beauty.

Yet modern man is in danger of letting his own conceit blot out this revelation of God. Instead of praying for rain, we talk about making rain ourselves. We seed clouds, but who made the clouds? Jesus introduces us to a character much like ourselves. "The ground of a certain rich man brought forth plentifully; and he thought within himself, saying, What shall I do, because I have no room where to bestow my fruits? . . . I will pull down my barns, and build greater; and there will I bestow all my fruits and my goods" (LUKE 12:16, 18). I—I—I; My—My—My. There is no sense of God. God the Creator he does not see.

Second, God reveals Himself through people. Through Moses we glimpse God's law, Amos showed us His justice, Hosea His love, and Micah His ethical standards. Someone was kind when we were sick, helped in time of trouble, friendly when we were lonely. Someone we had wronged forgave in a spirit of love. In all such acts a little of God is revealed unto us. You understand God better because of the love of your mother, the consecrated life of some friend, the heroism of some Joan of Arc. Corporate worship is so much more rewarding because we learn from each other.

God's supreme revelation of Himself is in Christ. "He that hath seen me hath seen the Father." As Harry Webb Farrington sang:

I know not how that Bethlehem's Babe
Could in the Godhead be;
I only know the manger Child
Has brought God's life to me.

I know not how that Calvary's cross
A world from sin could free:
I only know its matchless love
Has brought God's love to me.

I know not how that Joseph's tomb
Could solve death's mystery:
I only know a living Christ
Our immortality.

As you read the four Gospels and see Jesus you begin to realize that you are actually seeing God.

One other way God reveals Himself. I have no name or explanation for it. We may call it the "still, small voice," or the impress of His spirit on

us. But I can testify that there are times, perhaps
rare times, when you feel you have received a direct
word from Him. Samuel heard God directly.

As we know God, so can we pray, "Hallowed be
thy name," that is, "Make us surer of Thee, O God,
that we may understand Thee more fully." And as
our minds are filled with God, as we steadily gaze
upon Him, the little sins which so easily beset us
lose their power over us, and we become both
willing and able to hear and obey Him. That condition we must meet in order to pray with power.

thy kingdom come

"THY KINGDOM COME" IS THE SECOND THING
for which Jesus told us to pray. The very word
"kingdom" is offensive to Americans. "Democracy"
is our word. We demand the right to govern ourselves. Kipling refers to us as a people among
whom each man "dubs his dreary brethren Kings."
Especially today do we rebel against dictators and
totalitarianism. In fact, some of us assert the right
of self-rule even to the point of dethroning God.

But we need to be reminded that in one sense
God's kingdom has already come. His laws govern
the universe with absolute authority. The scientist

knows the law of God. He sees it in the precision of the cosmos. The physician will tell you there are certain laws of health. To obey them is to have health—to disobey them is to die. The psychiatrist understands that a man's pattern of thinking must be along right lines. To turn off the track is to become unbalanced. Even the sociologist teaches us that the good of one is the good of all. We are bound together in a common brotherhood, which is a law of God.

God established His kingdom on earth, which means His law and His rule. It is here right now. *Whether we like it or not, His rule is upon us.* As the Prophet said in the long ago: "The soul that sinneth, it shall die" (EZEKIEL 18:4).

We see the capitol building of our state. We know the governor and members of the legislature. We think of how man makes his laws. Yet any and every law of my state can be repealed or amended. There will be other governors and legislators.

Not so with the laws of God. I could rebel against God's law of gravitation and step out the window of a high building. But I would only destroy myself. I would not change the law. So I go down on an elevator. Is that not overcoming God's law with man's mechanical genius? No. Suppose the cable of the elevator breaks. It has happened. And the very fact that the elevator makers use such strong cables and regularly inspect them is a recognition of God's law and obedience to it.

This world is God's kingdom. It is under His sovereign rule and power, controlled by laws. However, in foolish disobedience, man rushes on to destroy himself. Will we ever come to our senses? Will we ever recognize the law of God to the point of surrender and obedience to it? There are many who say no. They are so depraved, so corrupted by egoism and so blinded by pride, that they cannot see the right way and have not the will to obey, even if they could.

Thus on every hand we hear destruction predicted for the world. But Jesus said pray, *"Thy kingdom come."* Surely He believed not only in its possibility but in the actual event.

One night Jesus locked the door of His little carpenter's shop for the last time. He must be about His Father's business. That business was to bring God's kingdom on earth. The text of His very first sermon was, "The kingdom of heaven is at hand" (MATTHEW 4:17). That was the one theme of His

26

preaching all the way. He never lost His faith, and even on the resurrection side of the grave He talked to His disciples of the kingdom of God (ACTS 1:3).

As we pray, "Thy kingdom come," it is well to underscore the word "come." It is so much easier to pray, "Thy kingdom go." It is not nearly as hard to pray for the conversion of Africa and to give offerings for missions as it is to face up honestly to our own sins, to repent and change our ways.

It is easier to crusade piously for world peace than it is to forgive someone who has done us wrong or whom we have wronged. David Livingstone sought out the savage with the Word of God, but first he dedicated himself. Even the last day of his life he wrote in his diary, *"My Jesus, my King, my Life, my All, I again dedicate my whole self to Thee."*

There is a verse of Scripture that literally haunts me. I have the blessed privilege of preaching to many people. During the very week I am writing these words I am visiting in Columbia, the capital city of South Carolina, preaching in one of the largest churches of the state. Each night the great auditorium is filled and many are being turned away. Yet there is something much harder than preaching to others. St. Paul said: "But I keep under my body, and bring it into subjection: lest that by any means, when I have preached to others, I myself should be a castaway" (I CORINTHIANS 9:27). If the greatest Christian preacher of all time was in danger of becoming a castaway, how much more so is it true for me.

"Thy kingdom come." This means that I look into my own heart and plead for God's cleansing power. It means that I bow before Him in faith and true obedience.

Archibald Rutledge told the story of meeting a Negro turpentine worker whose faithful dog had died a few moments earlier in a great forest fire because he would not desert his master's dinner pail, which he had been told to watch. With tears in his face, the old Negro said: "I always had to be careful what I tol' him to do, 'cause I knowed he'd do it." That is what this prayer means.

Jesus said, "The kingdom of heaven is like unto a merchant man, seeking goodly pearls: who, when he had found one pearl of great price, went and sold all that he had, and bought it" (MATTHEW 13:45, 46). The pearls he sold meant a lifetime of labor. They represented all he had. Yet the one pearl was worth all else. So, to really pray, "Thy kingdom come," means I am willing to surrender everything I possess in order to possess God. *God demands our all or nothing at all.*

It is so much easier for me to talk about the sins of the world, the corruption of government, for instance, or the evils of liquor, or of filthy literature and motion pictures, or the honky-tonks around town, or the heathens in China. But before I pray about where God's kingdom is needed, first let it come to me.

Jonathan Edwards, one of the most effective preachers America ever knew, so prayed. He said, "I go out to preach with two propositions in mind. First, every person ought to give his life to Christ. Second, whether or not anyone else gives Him his life, I will give Him mine."

The Apostle said, "Let all bitterness, and wrath, and anger, and clamor, and evil speaking, be put away from you, with all malice: And be ye kind one to another, tenderhearted, forgiving one another, even as God for Christ's sake hath forgiven you" (EPHESIANS 4:31, 32). That is what the coming of God's kingdom means for us, and when it comes, then we can spread it forth with power. Unrighteous people are not very powerful crusaders for a righteous world. As the spiritual tells us: "It ain't my brother, it ain't my sister, it's me, O Lord, standing in the need of prayer."

"Thy kingdom come." When that prayer is answered, then we shall have no doubt of the power of God's kingdom to cover the earth.

thy will be done in earth, as it is in heaven

TO PRAY WITH POWER, JESUS TEACHES US, WE must first get God in our minds and recognize His sovereignty. We must pray, "Thy will be done." Right there many people hesitate, lose their nerve, and turn away from God. I think I know why.

When I was studying psychology in college I worked out a number of word tests which I would use on my congregations. For example, say to a person the word "Christmas" and ask that person the first word which comes into his mind. I would get such answers as Santa Claus, decorations, gifts, etc. Rarely would Christ be mentioned. So I would conclude we had commercialized and paganized the Lord's birthday. I think the test was valid, with some limitations.

Well, let's try it on ourselves. I will name a

phrase and check your first thought. "Will of God."
What does that bring to your mind? The death of
a loved one, or some great disaster, or severe suffering from some incurable disease, or some hard
sacrifice. Most people will think of some dark picture in relation to the will of God.

Perhaps one cause is our Lord's prayer in Gethsemane, "Nevertheless not my will, but thine be
done" (LUKE 22:42). And from His surrender
to God's will we see Christ walking up Calvary and
being nailed to a cross. So God's will and crosses
come to be synonymous terms for us.

However, we can go back further. There was
Job. He lost his wealth, his children were killed,
he suffered in body, and his wife deserted him. Job
associated all those disasters with God, so he said,
"The Lord gave, and the Lord hath taken away;
blessed be the name of the Lord" (JOB 1:21). So,
when our hearts are broken we say "It is the Lord's
will." Naturally we shrink from such a will.

It seems to be a general belief that the will of
God is to make things distasteful for us, like taking
bad-tasting medicine when we are sick, or going
to the dentist. Yet we think we would be much
happier if we disregarded God's will. We never

say, "No, I forever turn my back on God's will." But we do say, "For the time being I will back my own judgment and follow my own will."

Somebody needs to tell us that sunrise is also God's will. There is the time of harvest, the harvest which will provide food and clothes for us, without which life could not be sustained on earth. God ordered the seasons, they are His will. In fact, the good things in life far outweigh the bad. *There are more sunrises than cyclones.*

I live comfortably during the winter in an automatically steam-heated house. Long before I was born God stored up in the ground the gas which is now being piped into my home for my good. I might say that cold winter freezes are God's will, but I must also know that the warmth God has provided is also His will. Whether you shrink from His will or gratefully surrender to it depends on how you look at it.

Jesus said, "Thy will be done in earth, as it is in heaven." "As in heaven," He said. What do you think of when the word "heaven," comes to your mind? You think of peace, plenty, perfect joy, the absence of pain and suffering and tears. John saw it all and recorded his vision in Revelation 21. That is what we want here and now in our own lives. *Jesus says that is God's will for us.*

Before you can pray, "Thy will be done," you must believe it is the best and happiest way. However, sometimes we surrender to the immediate, while God considers life as a whole. For example, here are two boys in school. The will of the teacher is that they spend hours in hard studying. One of the boys rebels against the unpleasant work. He wants to be happy, so he goes to a picture show. Maybe he quits school to go his carefree way.

The other boy sticks to his studies, difficult though they may be. Look at those same two boys ten or twenty years later. The carefree boy is now bound and limited by his own ignorance. He endures hardships and embarrassment caused by his lack of training. The other boy is freer, happier, and finds life easier and more rewarding because he was properly prepared.

There was Joseph, the darling of his father Jacob's heart. Home was for him a place of great joy. But jealousy welled up in his brothers, who put Joseph in a dark well, and later sold him into slavery. Later those same brothers stood before him in need. Joseph said to them: "Be not grieved, nor

34

angry with yourselves, that ye sold me hither: for God did send me before you to preserve life" (GEN-ESIS 45:5).

Surely Joseph's way was hard. But he kept his faith, never giving up, and at the end he could look back and see, as we read in "Hamlet," "There's a divinity that shapes our ends." *Out of the surrender of our Lord in Gethsemane did come a cross, but beyond the cross lay an empty tomb and a redeemed world.*

Sometimes it is not God who leads us through deep valleys and dark waters. It may be man's ignorance and folly. But even then we can feel His presence, for out of our mistakes God can make something beautiful. God did not bring Job's tragedies. But because of Job's faith God could use those tragedies for Job's final good. It is wonderful what God can do with a broken heart when we give Him all the pieces.

To pray, "Thy will be done," is really an enlistment for action. In 1792 William Carey preached a sermon on the text: "Enlarge the place of thy tent, and let them stretch forth the curtains of thine habitations: spare not, lengthen thy cords, and strengthen thy stakes" (ISAIAH 54:2).

35

It was one of the most influential sermons ever preached on this earth, because the result was the birth of the Baptist Missionary Society, the story of which a hundred books could not begin to tell. In that sermon Carey made his famous statement: "Expect great things from God, attempt great things for God."

But here is the important point. He not only preached about missions, he gave up all he had and went himself to India as a missionary. He prayed literally, "in earth as it is in heaven." He meant the whole earth and he dedicated his life in answer to his own prayer.

Who knows but that if the money we have spent on atomic bombs had been used in medical research, we would not now have the answer not only for polio but also for cancer, arthritis, and many other diseases. We feel compelled to maintain our vast program of defense. Yet whose fault is it? If we had spent on Christian missions in Japan the cost of one battleship which the Japanese sank at Pearl Harbor, we might never have had that war. If we had maintained a Christian spirit in Germany after World War I, we might never have heard of Hitler.

Actually, God's will is on earth. It is operating in

your very life. For example, you did not decide in what century you would be born. You were not free to choose who your parents would be. The color of your skin, your sex, your physical appearance, all were decided by a higher will, God's will.

And God's will is in operation in our lives. There is a purpose for your life. I believe no person is an accident. Before you were born on the earth you existed in the mind of God. You can rebel against God, but ultimately you will be totally defeated. You can endure life as it comes, and find no joy and peace in it. Or you can choose the will of God and make His will your will.

As Tennyson put it: *"Our wills are ours, we know not how; our wills are ours, to make them thine."*

How can I know the will of God for my life? Many will never know, because God does not reveal Himself to triflers. No one can walk into His holy presence on hurrying feet. If you merely pray, "Lord, this is my will, I hope You will approve," you are wasting your breath. Only those who sincerely want God's will, and have faith enough in Him to dedicate themselves to His will, can ever know it. To pray, "Lord, show me Thy will. If I like it I will accept it," is a futile prayer. You must accept it before you know it. Whether or not you can do that depends on your opinion of God.

To the sincere, God reveals His will in many ways. Often we learn through the process we call insight. A psychiatrist once said to me, "Either a person has insight or he hasn't. It isn't something which can be learned." But it is something which God can give.

I have talked with people who have baffling problems. Maybe they have tossed many weary hours trying to sleep, but could not because of a problem. In the quietness of the pastor's study we have talked about God and His love and concern for us. After a prayer, we talked about the problem. And not once, but many times, I have seen a light on their faces, as suddenly the answer came, a solution came to mind. I say God gave them insight. Sometimes it is called the "inner light."

God may reveal His will through the advice of others, through circumstances, through the experiences of history, through the discovery of His laws by scientific investigation, through the voice of His church. Certainly we see His will as we study the life and teachings of Jesus.

I have a little radio that I carry in my bag. At home I can hear any station in Atlanta I turn to. But if I get too far away the voice of the station is blotted out. It is the same radio—the station is broadcasting with the same power. But I have gone too far away. Many miss God's voice because they are too far away from Him.

The assurance that you are within the will of God does more to eliminate the fears and worries of life than any other one thing. "In His will is our peace." Surrender to His will takes the dread out of tomorrow. We know, absolutely we know, that if we do His will today, tomorrow will be according to His will. I am not a fatalist, instead I can say with the Psalmist, "I have not seen the righteous forsaken" (37:25). Obedience to His will today means that God assumes the responsibility for our tomorrow.

So, Jesus teaches us that the first three petitions of our prayer must be with our eyes fixed firmly on God. There is a place in prayer to talk about our own needs, and our Lord assures us it is right to pray for ourselves, but first God must fill our minds before we come to our own problems. Then we are ready to talk about what we want Him to do for us.

GIVE US THIS DAY
OUR DAILY BREAD

IN THE MIDDLE OF THE LORD'S PRAYER THERE
is a distinct division. You see it in the pronouns.
In the first three petitions we are taught to say
"Thy": "Thy name," "Thy kingdom," "Thy will."
But in the last three petitions are "us" and "our."
First, we think of God, then we can rightfully
think of ourselves.

And the very first petition our Lord permits us
to pray for ourselves is the one we really want to
pray. In fact, it is the one we must pray if we plan
to stay alive. "Give us this day our daily bread." By
that He means simply the physical necessities of
life.

Many of the early church fathers, such as Je-
rome, Origen, and Augustine, taught that this
petition was for the same bread which Jesus refers
to when He says, "I am the bread of life" (JOHN
6:35). They felt it was wrong to pray for material
blessings. And that idea persists to this day.

But why try to spiritualize this petition? After all, even a saint must eat. Even our very prayers would die on our lips if we did not have food to sustain our bodies. Jesus preached to the people, He healed the sick, He forgave their sins, and He also used His marvelous power to feed them real bread.

Study our Lord's life. You will see He knew something about the everyday struggle to make ends meet. He knew the meaning of the widow's two mites, of what a disaster the loss of a coin might be, or wearing clothes which were patched. He knew about shopping in the grocery store to try to stretch a budget to feed the family. He talks about the housewife who must buy two birds which sold for a penny.

Even on the resurrection side of the grave our Lord was concerned with bread. We see Him walking home with two of His friends on that first Easter Sunday. He spoke hope to their hearts and He also took time to sit at the table with them. In fact, the Bible says, "He took bread, and blessed it, and brake, and gave to them" (LUKE 24:30).

In the gray dawn of the morning we see Him on the seashore. His disciples had been fishing all night. Now they were coming in, and the Lord was prepared for them. What did He prepare? A prayer meeting? They needed prayer. A majestic and overwhelming revelation of Himself? They had lost faith in Him. No, He prepared breakfast.

The risen, resplendent Christ cooking breakfast! Though His feet were bruised, He walked over a rocky beach to gather firewood. Though His hands were nail-pierced, He cleaned fish. He knew that the fishermen would be hungry.

He knows we have groceries to buy, rent or payments to make on our houses, clothes that are necessary, expenses for the children in school, bills of every sort to meet. Not only that, He knows we have desires and wants beyond our bare necessities. We are not wild beasts. We want some of the pleasant things of life.

Much better than we, He knew that the body and the soul are an inseparable unity. Just as worry and fear can affect the body and make one sick, so one's physical condition can affect a man's outlook on life, his religious faith, his moral conduct. *The God who made our bodies is concerned about the needs of our bodies and He is anxious for us to talk with Him about our physical needs.*

Every morning the sun rises to warm the earth.

If it were to fail to shine for just one minute, all life on the earth would die. The rains come to water the earth. There is fertility in the soil, life in the seeds, oxygen in the air. The providence of God is about us in unbelievable abundance every moment. But so often we just take it for granted.

Dr. John Witherspoon was a great American and a man of God. He was one of the signers of the Declaration of Independence and president of the College of New Jersey which later became Princeton. He lived about two miles from the college and drove over in his buggy each day.

One morning a neighbor came excitedly into his study and said, "Dr. Witherspoon, you must join me in giving thanks to God for His providence in saving my life. As I was driving this morning the horse ran away and the buggy was smashed to pieces on the rocks, but I escaped unharmed."

"Why," answered Dr. Witherspoon, "I can tell you a far more remarkable providence than that. I have driven over that road hundreds of times. My horse never ran away, my buggy never was smashed, I was never hurt. God's providence has been for me even more remarkable than it has been for you."

All of us know so well Maltbie D. Babcock's verse:

Back of the loaf is the snowy flour,
And back of the flour the mill,
And back of the mill is the wheat
and the shower,
And the sun and the Father's will.

The same is true of everything you have—the new television set you enjoy, or the nice car in which you take such great pride, or the home in which you live, or the clothes you are now wearing. All of those things come from the earth which God made. He put those things within our reach because He knew we would want them and would enjoy them. Long before you were born, God answered your prayer for material blessings. "Give us this day our daily bread" is a prayer that has truly been answered. It is also a recognition of what He has already done. I like to read that story of Jesus in the wilderness. Matthew tells us there were five thousand people with Him (14:21). They were hungry, and the Lord wanted them fed. The disciples surveyed the situation, and all the food they could find was a little boy's lunch of five loaves and two small fishes.

The disciples felt this was too little with which to bother. With such meager resources, there was no need to try. But watch the Lord's actions. No complaint from Him about not having more. Instead, the first thing He did was to give thanks. Then He started using what He had. He began breaking and passing the food.

To the astonishment of all, what He had was enough to feed everyone. In fact, they had more than they needed, and there were twelve baskets of food left over. The people were so amazed that immediately they tried to take Him by force and make Him a king (JOHN 6:5–15).

If today we would begin to be thankful for what we have, and use it as best we can, God would give us insight as to how we could multiply what we have to cover every need of our lives, and have a lot left over. We would be so blessed that we would fall before Him as our Lord and King.

and forgive us our debts, as we forgive our debtors

JESUS GIVES US SIX PETITIONS TO MAKE. THREE concern God, and three are for ourselves. All six of them are of supreme importance, yet there is one of the six on which He turns the spotlight. He does not find it necessary to emphasize that we pray that God's name be hallowed, or that God's kingdom come, or that His will be done, vital as those are.

He does not emphasize our need for bread, yet without bread we would all die. But after the Lord's Prayer is completed, our Lord feels He should turn back and lift one petition out for special comment. "And forgive us our debts, as we forgive our debtors" is the prayer He spotlights. He says, "But if ye forgive not men their trespasses, neither will your Father forgive your trespasses" (MATTHEW 6:15).

It isn't that God forgives on an exchange basis. Our forgiveness of others is not a condition of God's forgiveness of us. Rather is it a condition of our ability to receive the forgiveness of God. We are told by Shakespeare, "The quality of mercy is not strain'd, it droppeth as the gentle rain from heaven." But I could cover a plant with a sheet of iron and the rain could not get to it. So, I can surround my soul with an unforgiving spirit and completely block the forgiving mercy of God.

A wrong spirit toward another person may or

may not hurt him, but it is certain to destroy my own soul. Booker T. Washington understood it when he said, "I will not permit any man to narrow and degrade my soul by making me hate him."

I remember a scene from "Amos and Andy." There was a big man who would slap Andy across the chest whenever they met. Finally, Andy got enough of it and said to Amos, "I am fixed for him. I put a stick of dynamite in my vest pocket and the next time he slaps me he is going to get his hand blown off." Andy had not realized that at the same time his own heart would be blown out. The dynamite of hatred may inflict some injury on someone else and also blow out our own heart.

The words "forgiving" and "forgiven" are inseparable. They go together. At the death of Queen Caroline, Lord Chesterfield said a sad thing: "And unforgiving, unforgiven dies."

On the cross our Lord prays, "Father, forgive them; for they know not what they do" (LUKE 23:34). Often what we deplore is the innocent act of some person. But for us there is an even more important reason for not holding a grudge: "for *we* know not." If we understood the person, usually our judgments would not be so harsh.

With our limited understanding of each other, it is a fearful thing to set ourselves up as judges. The Bible says, "Vengeance is mine; I will repay, saith the Lord" (ROMANS 12:19). If we are wise we will leave that business to God. Somewhere I read these lines:

> Has God deserted Heaven,
> And left it up to you,
> To judge if this or that is right,
> And what each one should do?
>
> I think He's still in business,
> And knows when to wield the rod,
> So when you're judging others,
> Just remember, you're not—God.

"As we forgive," He told us to pray.

A couple had gone to an orphanage to adopt a child. One little fellow particularly appealed to them. They talked to him about all the things they would give him—clothes, toys, a good home. None of these things seemed to appeal to the boy much. So finally they asked him, "What do you want most?" He replied, "I just want somebody to love me."

That is what we all want. Deep in every human

heart is a hunger for love. Loneliness is a cross for more people than we realize. Yet people are hard to love. They have so many faults, they say things they shouldn't, many have antagonistic and unattractive spirits. Yet Jesus told us to pray, "Forgive as we forgive." This is the only petition He emphasized. Maybe it is the hardest one to say.

"For if you forgive not men their trespasses"—debts—sins—! Either of those words could be used, maybe all three express what our Lord had in mind. Debts suggest failure to discharge obligations, not merely financial. There are also such debts as the debts of friendship, citizenship, etc.

"Trespasses" indicates the unlawful use of another's property. We see signs, "No Trespassing," and we know that the sign means "Keep Off." Our friends also trespass on our time, they trespass on our name and do it harm when they talk about us wrongfully. In many ways do friends trespass on us.

Sin indicates vice and wrong conduct. And we see a lot in our friends. In fact, the more you study the faults of your friends, the harder it becomes to offer this prayer, "as we forgive others." And sometimes we invest our love in friends only to be bitterly disappointed.

Sometimes we might feel like Sir Walter Raleigh who, just a few hours before his death, wrote his wife: "To what friend to direct thee I know not, for mine have left me in the true time of trial." Some people have been so deeply hurt that they cannot feel that Tennyson was right when he said:

> I hold it true, whate'er befall,
> I feel it, when I sorrow most;
> 'Tis better to have loved and lost,
> Than never to have loved at all.

But notice carefully that Jesus said, "Forgive us our debts." He directs our attention first to our own debts—trespasses—sins. The faults of those about us are also in us. Maybe not exactly the same ones, but probably worse ones. He did not tell us to pray, "Forgive us *if* we have sinned." There is definitely no *if* about it.

Let us honestly ask ourselves some questions and answer them: "What is my worst failure? That is, wherein have I not lived up to my obligations?" Second, "What is one way I have mistreated another person?" Third, "What is one sin I have

52

committed?" Each of us has some answer for each of those questions. We all stand convicted.

But also, do our friends have an answer for those questions? They, too, are guilty. Now, the supreme point is: If you will be willing to forgive them, then you will be able to receive God's forgiveness of you. It seems to be a good bargain for me. How about you?

and lead us not into temptation, but deliver us from evil

OUR LORD GIVES US THREE PRAYERS TO PRAY for ourselves. One is for the present, "Give us this day our daily bread." One looks both to the past and to the present, "Forgive us our sins." The third prayer looks to the future. As to our need to pray for bread and for forgiveness we are in agreement, but most of us take a view different from that of our Lord as to the prayer we should pray for tomorrow.

As we look to the future what is it we need to pray about? What do we fear and shrink from the most? For some the answer is sickness, so we ask God to keep us well, we are interested in preventive medicine, we take out sickness and hospitalization insurance. We fear poverty, so we save for the rainy days. Others fear suffering. We worry about the possibility of being hurt.

We fear unpopularity and criticism, we fear old age, we fear death. But when Christ tells us what to pray about for the future, He mentions not one of these things. The one thing we need to pray about for the future is the possibility of doing wrong. The one fear we should have above all fears is that in the midst of temptation we shall slip.

But we take less seriously our Lord's prayer for the future than we take any of the other five petitions. We are not afraid of temptation. In fact, we are so confident of being able to command our own selves that we make temptation a constant companion.

There is an old story of a man who had been the victim of strong drink but who had reformed and apparently was the conqueror of his evil habit. However, when he drove into town, he continued to hitch his horse at the post in front of the town saloon. Eventually he fell into his old ways again. Had he had a healthy fear of temptation he would have changed his hitching post.

Temptation most often comes first as a thought. In the secret places of our minds we dramatize and act out the thought. We read books that describe wickedness, we play with emotional dynamite as if it were a harmless toy. We get ourselves into dangerous situations and enjoy being there. We keep the wrong company. When we go about work or pleasure, some enticing voice may whisper, "Brother, lend me your soul." We might hesitate to give away a dime, even if we have a pocketful of coins, but we risk our souls though we know it may be for eternity. When it is temptation we face we are foolishly brave.

Not so with Jesus. He tells us to fear the temptation of the morrow more than any other thing. Our very strength is our greatest weakness because the overconfidence in our strength leads to our downfall. We are afraid of our weaknesses and guard against them. But we take chances with our strengths, and that is where we lose. *"Wherefore let him that thinketh he standeth take heed lest he fall"* (I CORINTHIANS 10:12).

What is temptation? First, it is an inducement to evil. Read the third chapter of Genesis and you find a story that has been repeated in some form in the life of every person who has come after Adam and Eve.

The serpent said to Eve, "Hath God said, Ye shall not eat of every tree in the garden?" Eve replied, "All except one. If we eat of that one we shall die." The serpent told her it would not hurt her. "In fact, if you eat of that tree you will know more, you will have a larger and freer life."

Here her inclinations began to struggle with her reason and conscience. The "Thou-shalt-not" of God and the alluring promise of forbidden pathways came in conflict. Thus temptation was set up.

Second, temptation means a test or a trial. It is like a fork in the roadway of life, where one must decide a direction to take, and action to carry out, a character to be. A mother whose son has been killed may be tempted to become bitter and harsh. One who is facing a difficult life situation may be tempted to escape by getting drunk.

One who is destined to a bed of suffering or the chair of an invalid may be tempted to self-pity. When someone has treated us unfairly there is the temptation to hate, spite, or resentment. One who has prospered is tempted to vanity and self-love. The successful is tempted to seek undue power.

When he was a boy in school Napoleon wrote an essay on the dangers of ambition. Yet his own ambition wrecked his life. Moses was noted for his meekness. In fact, the Bible says he was the meekest man on earth (NUMBERS 12:3). Yet, in a moment, when he tried to usurp the power of God by striking the rock, he lost his chance to enter the Promised Land. Simon Peter was noted for his impulsive courage. Yet it was through failure of his greatest strength that he denied his Lord.

A man is no stronger than his weakest moment, and every man has an Achilles' heel, a point of vulnerability. We cannot escape temptation because we are endowed with freedom of choice. And since no person has an iron will, every one is in danger of falling. We can choose between good and evil, between being true and false, between being brave and cowardly, between being generous and selfish. And the very freedom of choice becomes in itself temptation.

Many stumble at the interpretation of this petition, feeling that God would not lead one of His children into temptation. *But God is concerned with the creation of character, and to create character He gives us freedom of choice.* Otherwise we would be nothing more than mere puppets.

Life would be much simpler if we had no such freedom. Thomas Henry Huxley once declared: "If some great Power would agree to make me think always what is true and do what is right on condition of being turned into a sort of clock, I should instantly close with the bargain. The only freedom I care about is the freedom to do right; the freedom to do wrong I am ready to part with." But one freedom requires the other, thus our temptation.

God gave to each of us a free will, yet the very possession of our freedom should so frighten us that in every possible way we should throw safeguards around it. We should be very afraid of any circumstance that might mean our downfall.

Jesus tells us: "If thy right hand offend thee, cut it off" (MATTHEW 5:30). He may mean those words literally, for certainly it would be better to lose one's hand than to lose one's soul. However, I think He means by "the hand" the work of the hand— "Whatsoever thy hand findeth to do. . . ." If your daily job brings you into tempting situations, better to give up the job even at the cost of sacrifice.

Again He says, "If thy right eye offend thee, pluck it out" (MATTHEW 5:29). Probably what He means by "the eye" is the things you have your eye set on—your goals and ambitions. One can be so set on success, social or material, that he reaches the point where he demands "success at any price." If the direction of your life is a peril to your soul, better to try another road.

Elizabeth Barrett Browning understood it when she said:

I was too ambitious in my deed,
And thought to distance all men in success,
Till God came on me, marked the place, and said,
"Ill-doer, henceforth keep within this line,
Attempting less than others"—and I stand,
And work among Christ's little ones, content.

"Lead us not into temptation" is a prayer that makes us look at our choices, seeing beyond our goals to the final destination of the road we would travel. This is a prayer that can be answered and is answered in many ways. Sometimes it is answered by God's direct providence, by what we call coincidence. Why is it you missed getting a certain job or opportunity? Maybe it was God intervening. At times this prayer is answered by what we call insight. In certain hard moments of decision we feel, deep inside ourselves, the right course to take.

Most of all is this prayer answered by the inner strength which God gives to all who sincerely desire it. In despair we sometimes throw up our hands. We feel caught in an entanglement of circumstances, or by the chains of some habit, or by our own inherent weakness. We say, "What's the use? I cannot do better." But when we sincerely desire to rise above our temptations and look to God for deliverance, a new inner strength becomes ours, a new spirit of confidence rises within us.

For thine is the kingdom, and the power,
and the glory, for ever.

One of the most sublime verses in the Bible is tucked away in the little Book of Jude: "Now unto him that is able to keep you from falling, and to present you faultless before the presence of his glory with exceeding joy" (verse 24). Through this verse you begin to realize you are made for victory instead of defeat, you are to overcome evil rather than be overcome by it, and triumphantly you declare with the Apostle: "I can do all things through Christ which strengthened me" (PHILIPPIANS 4:13).

The biggest lie of the devil is that we have to sin.

61

"After all, you are human," he says, and thereby our high resolves are destroyed. We surrender and quit the struggle. One takes a very different view when he becomes acquainted with a Power beyond human power. "I can do all things through Christ which strengtheneth me." That is a tremendously powerful truth, once we possess it.

There is a little story we read as children about the little engine climbing the hill. As it puffed and struggled it kept saying, "I think I can, I think I can, I think I can." Nothing is ever accomplished by the person who says, "I think I cannot," or "It is beyond me." *Just to say, "I can," is to gain immediate power. But to add two words and say, "I can in Him" is to multiply your power manyfold.*

I read recently of an experiment made by a psychologist. We are familiar with those gripping machines. You put in a penny and try your grip. Three men tried their grip, with no suggestion from the psychologist, and the average grip was 101 pounds. Then the three were hypnotized and the psychologist told each, "You cannot grip, because you are weak." Under the power of that suggestion their average grip fell from 101 pounds to only 29.

With the three men still under the power of hypnosis, the psychologist told them to grip again, but this time he told them. "Now you can grip." Their strength was five times greater when they said, "I can," than it was when they said, "I cannot."

Study the lives of those we call saints, those who have attained unusual spiritual power, and you will find their secret right at this point. They sinned, but they never surrendered to sin. They never accepted failure as final. They never ceased to look forward with confidence. They kept saying, "I can in Him." And to the utmost of their power was added His power.

The same power is available for any one of us. You may look into a past of shame and defeat, but I tell you that you can look into a future of peace and victory. "Only believe, only believe; all things are possible, only believe." That is more than just a little chorus. It is the Christian faith.

What amazing confidence did our Lord have in us! C. F. Andrews reminds us of on old legend that tells us that when Jesus returned to heaven He was asked by an angel: "What have you left behind to carry out the work?" Jesus answered: "A little band of men and women who love Me." "But what if they fail when the trial comes? Will all You have done be defeated?" "Yes," said Jesus, "if they fail, all I have done will be defeated."

"Is there nothing more?" "No," said Jesus, "there is nothing more." "What then?" Jesus quietly replied, "They will not fail."

With a confidence like that we can see the complete victory of God in our own lives and our world. As we face tomorrow we can triumphantly declare:

FOR THINE IS THE KINGDOM, AND THE POWER, AND THE GLORY, FOREVER. AMEN.